Keto Diet Slow Cooker Cookbook 2019

Delicious Ketogenic Diet Recipes to Rapid Weight Loss, Save Time& Money, and Improve Your Lifestyle

Jennifer Green

_____

Table of Contents

Introduction

Greetings! Jennifer Green here. First, I would like to congratulate and thank you for choosing this book, "***Keto Diet Slow Cooker Cookbook to Rapid Weight Loss, Save Time & Money, and Improve Your Lifestyle-Most Delicious Slow Cooking Low Carb High Fat Ketogenic Diet Recipes Made for Your Crock-Pot***".

This book suits individuals of any body weight or body shape! We've helped more than 400,000 people lose their weight and keep a healthier lifestyle. It will also help you!

How many times have you ever failed losing weight? Do you still have the courage to try again and want to lose weight? Do you want to be healthier, with fewer illnesses, be more attractive, and still be able to have delicious foods?

How often you don't have the time to prepare a meal? Do you just want to put all the ingredients into a slow cooker, wait for the cooking process to end, and have delectable dinner after some hours? Keep reading, you will find all the answers in this book!

Follow the keto lifestyle with a slow cooker to prepare easy, healthy, and delicious meals that improve your overall health. The ketogenic diet emphasizes a low-carb, high fat, and adequate protein meal plan. With the keto diet, you will eat low-carb and high-fat foods. By imitating this diet, your body will enter into a state of ketosis. While in ketosis, your liver produces ketones to fuel your brain and muscles, instead of glucose. Normally, if carbs are the source of fuel, you can gain weight and be deprived of energy. Fortunately, this book offers a quick and easy guide on using the instant pot and keto diet.

By following a ketogenic diet, you will get many benefits, below are some of them:

No undernourishment.

Lose weight faster.

A stable energy level.

Increases endurance.

Improves blood profile indicators.

Reduces or eliminates the need for diabetic medications.

Regulates blood pressure without medication.

Eliminates insulin resistance.

Be wiser by increasing mental focus and clearing mental fog.

The recipes you will create using the slow cooker (Crock-Pot) are low in carbohydrates and can reduce weight. With these recipes, you certainly have a new meal every day for the next few weeks. You will also learn about the slow cooker and keto diet, such as:

1. **Everything About the Slow Cooker.**
2. **Brief Overview of the Ketogenic Diet.**
3. **Benefits of the Ketogenic Diet.**
4. **How Does a Slow Cooker Work.**
5. **Other Useful Advice and More!**
6. **A 7- Day Meal Plan**

Lastly, this book will open the splendid world of flavorsome foods to you. All the recipes are unique, delicious, easy to make, and with ingredients that are inexpensive. The final chapter provides a 7- day meal plan, which is a great start for your ketogenic journey. Consider this book not just your average cookbook but as your ally. This book is created for daily use; it contains a multitude of healthy and wonderful recipes you can enjoy each day.

The combination of the ketogenic diet and the slow cooker will help you to achieve the healthy lifestyle you have always dreamed about, and in a very short time, too. Slow cooker will save you too much time, and most important is that the recipes made by slow cooker have more nutrition value. You no need to be a chef or familiar with cooking, or like cooking. You can be just a newer of cooking without knowing any cooking skills. You will know how to make delicious foods by yourself only need you following this book step by step!

We have made this book very easy to follow. All of what we have known and experienced about ketogenic diet are here. The tips and essential knowledge of the ketogenic diet and Slow Cooker are just a few minutes of reading. This book is not just a good guide for your ketogenic diet, and it's not only for losing weight; we believe it will be your lifelong companion. The next few weeks will be full of amazing results.

Happy reading!

Chapter 1: Everything About the Ketogenic Diet

There are many low-carb diets available. One of the most popular is the "ketogenic diet". More and more people are turning to the ketogenic diet because of the various advantages this diet carries. The ketogenic diet is a powerful way to lose weight and offers multiple benefits leading to a healthy lifestyle that fad diets do not. In this chapter, you will learn everything you need to know about the ketogenic diet.

What is the Ketogenic Diet?

The ketogenic diet is a high-fat, moderate protein, low-carbohydrate diet. This diet concentrates on decreasing your carbohydrate intake and replacing it with healthy fats and proteins. Normally, your body burns carbohydrates to convert into glucose, which is then carried around your body and is essential for brain fuel. However, when your body has low amounts of carbohydrates, the liver will convert fat into fatty acids and ketone bodies. The ketone bodies then move into the brain and replace glucose as the primary energy source.

The ketogenic diet was created to reach a state of ketosis. Ketosis is a metabolic state where your body produces ketones. Ketones are produced by your liver and used as fuel toward your body and brain instead of glucose. To make ketones, you must consume a substantial number of carbs and a bare minimum amount of proteins. The traditional ketogenic diet contains a 4:1 ratio by weight of fat to combined protein and carbohydrate. This is accomplished by eliminating high-carbohydrate foods, such as starchy fruits, vegetables, breads, grains, pasta, and sugar while boosting the consumption of foods high in fats, such as nuts, cream, and butter. The bottom line is the ketogenic diet is a low-carb diet useful in burning body fat.

Benefits of the Ketogenic Diet.

The ketogenic diet comes with many positive benefits. For beginners, it has been used to treat epileptic seizures and various other diseases, including cancer and Alzheimer's. Overall, the ketogenic diet can be used to improve and enhance your health by preventing and controlling the substances in your body. Here are some of the benefits of the ketogenic diet:

1. Weight Loss

The ketogenic diet focuses on keeping carbs to a minimum. Studies have proven that ketogenic practitioners lose weight easier and faster, compared to other people. Why? Because on a ketogenic diet, you drastically reduce the number of carbohydrates in every meal.

When you begin to consume fewer carbohydrates, the excess water in your body will shed. Thereby, reducing the levels of insulin, which directly affect your sodium levels, cultivating weight loss.

2. Diminish Your Appetite

Following a low-carb diet can alleviate your hunger. The worst side effect of this diet is feeling hungry. Hunger is the main reason why many people bail. However, when you follow the low-carb diet, your appetite is reduced. The more carbs you cut from your diet, the more protein and healthy fats is added. Thus, the fewer calories you consume. In other words, once you eliminate carbohydrates from your diet, your appetite will decrease and you end up consuming fewer calories, without even trying to eat less.

3. Decrease Blood Pressure

When your blood pressure is high or if you suffer from hypertension, you become prone to developing several health issues, like heart disease, kidney failure, or strokes. One of the most efficient ways to reduce your blood pressure is to maintain a low-carb diet. Successfully following a low-carb diet, your exposure to diseases is reduced. Research has also shown that by decreasing the consumption of carbohydrates leads to a significant reduction in blood pressure, thus reducing the risk of developing various diseases.

4. Improve Your HDL Cholesterol

HDL cholesterol is a special kind of protein that runs by transferring the "bad cholesterol" from your body and into your liver, where the cholesterol is either exerted or reused. When your HDL cholesterol level is high, your cholesterol deposits within your blood vessel walls, and this helps to prevent blockage that can provoke heart disease or heart pain. High-fat diets like the ketogenic diet are known for raising your blood vessels with HDL, which means you can reduce the risk of developing cardiovascular disease.

5. Improve Digestion

The ketogenic diet contains low carbs, low grains, and low sugars, which can significantly improve your digestion. When you consume carbs and sugars on a regular basis, it can result in gas, bloating, stomach pains, and constipation. Reducing sugars and carbohydrates in your diet can restore your digestive system.

6. Reduce Triglycerides

Triglycerides are also known as fat molecules. Increased levels of triglycerides are connected to heart health. Thus, it is important to lower triglyceride levels, which can be achieved with the ketogenic diet. The more carbohydrates you consume, the more triglycerides you will have in your blood, which can provoke heart disease. When you cut down carbohydrate consumption, the number of triglycerides in the body is dramatically reduced.

7. Increase Energy

A ketogenic diet can increase energy levels in multiple ways. It increases the mitochondrial function, and at the same time decreases the harmful radicals inside your body, thus making you feel more energetic and revitalized.

8. Improve Mental Health

The ketone bodies released when following ketogenic diet are directly connected to mental health. Research has shown that increased ketone levels can lead to stabilization of neurotransmitters, like dopamine and serotonin. This stabilization helps fight mood swings, depression, and other psychological issues.

Lose Weight Faster with the Ketogenic Diet than Other Diets

Obesity has become one of the largest health epidemics in the world. Many have tried multiple methods to fight obesity and excess weight, but their methods were not successful. To overcome obesity and lose weight, you must change your diet. The ketogenic diet has worked for many to preserve muscle mass and shed excess fat, without putting much effort.

The sole purpose of the ketogenic diet is to make your body enter a state of glycogen deprivation and maintain a state of ketosis, which is great for weight loss. Usually, in carb-based diets, carbohydrates are transformed into glucose, which is then used as the main fuel source for the body and brain. The remaining glucose converts to glycogen and gets stored in your liver for later use. When your glycogen levels are full, the excess is stored as fat, thus leading to weight gain.

This means that the main cause of weight gain is not eating fats, but the excessive consumption of carbs. Once you eliminate or reduce your carb intake and raise your fat intake, your body changes from burning carbs for energy to burning fats for energy. This means that the excess fats stored in your body will be burned for your energy source, consequently leading to weight loss.

Alongside, the ketogenic lifestyle also helps suppressing your appetite. This is largely because the foods you eat under the ketogenic diet, like fats and protein are quite filling; thus, you will stay full longer and don't feel the urge to eat often.

What Happens to Your Body Under the Ketogenic Diet?

When it comes to improving your health, losing weight, lowering health risks, gaining more energy, and mental clarity, t the ketogenic diet is so efficient because of ketosis, which is a status when your body produces ketones to provide energy for your brain and body. Usually, your body will break down carbohydrates and turn them into glucose for a source of fuel. However, when you adjust to a ketogenic diet, your body will go from storing carbohydrates to burning fat.

Over time, when you have successfully entered ketosis, your body will adapt to this new eating regime. During this short period of transitioning to ketogenic lifestyle, you may experience side effects.

Here is what may happen when your body enters the ketogenic diet:

1. Ketogenic Flu

In the first week of starting the ketogenic diet, it might be challenging for some. Your body may be used to relying mainly on glucose for energy, so it needs to evolve to using ketones for fuel. You may feel tired, unmotivated, and lethargic; this is generally caused by salt deficiency and dehydration that is promoted by the transitory increase in urinating. It also implies that your body will need to take more time to adjust to the different and new ingredients being digested and consumed.

Some of symptoms you may experience with Keto flu:

- Brain fogginess.
- Nausea.
- Cravings.
- Irritability.
- Sniffles.
- Coughing.
- Heart palpitations.
- Dizziness.
- Insomnia.

To help cope with the ketogenic flu, you should increase your water and salt intake, as this can prevent you from feeling lousy and tired.

2. Temporary Fatigue

For most dieters feeling fatigued and weak is one of the most common side effects in entering ketosis. This is mostly because your body is being deprived of carbohydrates, which is the only fuel source that your body has been used to. After a week or two, when your body has successfully adapted to burning fats, you will feel more energized and sense an improvement in mental clarity.

In the meantime, how can you cope with temporary fatigue? One thing you can do is take vitamin supplements. One essential nutrient your body always needs is Vitamin B5. If you do not have Vitamin B5, you will start to feel more fatigued or lethargic.

Vitamin B5 helps the adrenaline by boosting metabolism with more energy. Visit your local health store and purchase Vitamin B5, as it can help with temporary fatigue during your ketogenic journey.

3. Bad Breath

Something you should expect from your body under the ketogenic diet is stinky breath. It's not because the foods you eat cause bad breath. Bad breath is a common sign of ketosis because of the elevated levels of ketones in your blood. Notably, it's caused by a specific ketone known as acetone. This type of ketone usually leaves your body through your breath and urine, thus creating stinky breath.

Luckily, this symptom will last a short time. As with fatigue, bad breath will go away once your body is fully adapted to the ketogenic diet. Moreover, while waiting for your body to adjust to this diet, you can brush your teeth more frequently and use mouthwash more often.

4. Leg Cramps

Under the ketogenic diet, you may experience muscle cramps. They are common due to hyponatremia, which occurs when your level of sodium in the blood is low. To cope with muscle cramps, you can add an extra teaspoon of salt in your meals and stay well hydrated.

5. Headaches

As with many changes in your diet, headaches can occur for no reason. It is possibly you may become light-headed and start to have flu-like symptoms, which could occur over a few days. These headaches normally come about because of a mineral imbalance due to a change in diet. One way to resolve this is to add one-quarter teaspoon of salt to a glass of water and drink it. If you are just beginning the keto lifestyle, you should increase both your salt and water intake for the first couple of days to combat this effectively.

6. Difficulty Sleeping

Another symptom of embarking on the ketogenic diet is trouble sleeping. After cutting down on carbs, many novices to this diet often find themselves staying up later than usual, or frequently waking up at night. Remember, this is temporary. Over time, you will not have trouble sleeping. In fact, many people who remain on the ketogenic diet had their quality of sleep significantly improved.

7. Constipation

In your first week of the ketogenic diet, you may experience constipation because your body may need time to adjust to this new eating regime. To help you cope with this symptom, you can eat more vegetables loaded with fiber. This will keep your intestines moving and increase bowel movements. You can also drink more water to help fight dehydration, which is the contributing factor for constipation.

These are the most common signs of what your body could go through when embarking on the ketogenic diet. Not everyone experiences the same symptoms or may even encounter different symptoms. Do not feel discouraged or unmotivated about the diet. Remember, the symptoms will pass within a few weeks and you can reap the positive benefits from ketogenic lifestyle.

Dos and Don'ts of Ketogenic Diet

If you are not familiar with the Keto, mistakes can be made to to keep you from having good health and the benefits of this diet. To enhance the success with the ketogenic diet, here are some dos and don'ts about following the diet:

1. Don't increase your carb intake

The ketogenic diet is a low-carb diet, which means you should lower your carb intake. A specific number of carbs you should have in a diet is not there. Many people follow a diet where they consume 100 to 150 grams of carbs a day. To achieve ketosis, be sure that your carbohydrate intake is low.

Most keto dieters manage the state of ketosis by consuming between 20 to 100 grams of carbs a day.

2. Don't fear fat

If you are on a ketogenic diet, don't be scared of fat. Especially if you consume healthy fats like Omega-3s, monounsaturated fats, and saturated fats. This is encouraged in the ketogenic diet plan; a limit of 60 to 70% fat intake is best. To achieve these levels of fat, you must consume meat and healthy fats, such as olive oil, lard, butter, and coconut or alternatives on a daily basis.

3. Don't eat fast food

If you don't have time to cook, you may turn to fast foods. However, don't even think about it. Fast foods are incredibly unhealthy and can deter you from your keto journey. Fast foods contain too many harmful chemicals and preservatives, and some fast foods don't use real cheese, and meats that contain hidden sugars among other ingredients.

4. Do increase your protein intake

Protein is an essential and important nutrient that is needed for your body. It can soothe your appetite and burn fat more than any other nutrient. Generally, protein is said to be very effective in weight loss, increase muscle mass, and improve your body composition.

5. Do increase your sodium intake

By reducing carbohydrate consumption, your insulin levels fall, which in turn gets rid of extra sodium stored in your body, causing problems such as sodium deficiency. If your body experiences sodium deficiency, you might experience exhaustion, headaches, constipations, etc.

To relieve this problem, increase your sodium intake on a keto diet. Add a teaspoon of salt to daily meals or drink a glass of water with a ¼ teaspoon of salt mixed with it.

6. Do be patient

It is common nature for us to seek immediate gratification. When you start a diet, you may be discouraged to continue if you are not experiencing the benefits immediately. Losing weight and being healthy takes time. In order to do this, allow your body some time to start burning fat instead of glucose. It may take a few days or a couple of weeks, but be patient and don't bail on the diet.

Important Tips for Successful Ketogenic Journey

If you are just beginning the ketogenic journey, it may be hard for you to stick to this new eating regime, even if you know it's good for you. We are always influenced by unhealthy foods around us, and the accessibility to these foods make them difficult to pass up. Changing your diet is a long-term process; not something you do right off the bat. Here are some valuable tips for a successful ketogenic journey:

1. Gradually follow the ketogenic diet

A common mistake of many when starting the ketogenic diet is immediately eliminating carbohydrates. Doing this is not healthy for your body. While this may work in the short term, doing this can cause serious health problems over the long-term.

Give yourself time to maneuver into the keto lifestyle by making small but essential changes, like giving up one carb source every week or so. It's critical to give your body time to adjust to changes. An excellent way to overcome transition discomfort is to replace a healthy nutrient source to your diet for every unhealthy one. For example, if you use all-purpose flour, start substituting it with almond flour or coconut flour.

2. Drink plenty of water

When you start the ketogenic diet, your body will have a difficult time keeping the proper amount of water you need, so staying perfectly hydrated is the best way to go about it. Drink eight, 8-ounce glasses, which is equivalent to 2 liters every day. To know if you are well hydrated is to determine the color of your urine. Whenever your urine is light yellow or clear, you are properly hydrated.

3. Turn your favorite foods into ketogenic foods

Thinking of the foods you are not permitted to eat can become quite discouraging. Instead, learn keto-friendly versions of your favorite dishes. There are plenty of ketogenic cookbooks and internet recipes for tips and ideas on how to turn your favorite dishes into tasty ketogenic-friendly versions.

Following the ketogenic diet does not mean depriving yourself from your favorite meals, but about improving your diet and making it healthier. As the keto diet is high in fat, you will maintain all the flavors and texture from your favorite recipes. In many cases, the ketogenic diet has enhanced the flavor of many recipes.

4. Don't be afraid to ask for advice

If you have questions or confusions about the ketogenic diet, don't be afraid to ask for help. Ask professionals, ketogenic dieters, and maybe even certified nutritionists for advice, recipes, and experiences. You will be surprised by the experiences of others, and the information they share.

5. Be alert of alcohol consumption

You can still drink alcohol while on the keto diet without ruining the process. This is one of the great aspects of this diet. However, don't go overboard and drink all the time. It is preferred to go for unsweetened liquors, like scotch, tequila, vodka, whiskey, rum, and reduced-carb beer.

6. Be mindful of condiments and sauces

Not all condiments and sauces are healthy or ketogenic friendly. If you must use sauce and condiments, choose ones that are low in carbs, like soy sauce, lemon, salad dressings, mayonnaise, mustard, olive oil, and coconut oil (just to name a few).

In cases in which you can't tell if something is keto-friendly or not, you can always ask the server or chef. If they are not sure, it would be best to not use the sauce.

7. Be patient

Even though the ketogenic lifestyle is known for rapid weight loss, losing weight will take some time. Do not quit the diet when you are not experiencing quick results. Getting rid of fat will change throughout the day. Try not to get too worked up with a scale, instead be patient and trust that the ketogenic diet will help you lose weight.

8. Use vitamins and mineral salts

Foods high in carbohydrates contain many micronutrients, such as vitamins and minerals. When you stop eating carbohydrates, it can cause nutritional deficiency to your body. To help fight through this, you should use proper vitamins that can provide your body with nutrients.

9. Restock your fridge and pantry

If you are preparing to follow the ketogenic diet, the best way to begin is to rid the keto-unfriendly ingredients from your kitchen and restock with keto-friendly ones. This will make you more attentive and help you resist the urge to eat keto-unfriendly recipes.

Get everything you need to prepare your meals and plan ahead to avoid any inconveniences that may make you lose track of your diet.

What Foods Should Be on Your Plate?

There are specific guidelines for you to follow on the ketogenic diet. It was designed to help people with various diseases and for those looking to shed extra weight. It is best to take note of all the healthy and essential foods that are allowed on this diet.

Below is a list you should include on your menu:

Vegetables

You will eat tons of vegetables on the keto diet. However, you should be more attentive about the kinds of vegetables you consume. Eat vegetables high in nutrients and low in carbohydrates. Organic vegetables are the best, as they contain fewer chemicals and pesticides. The greatest advantage for eating non-starchy vegetables is that they do not raise your blood glucose levels, which would throw your ketosis off balance. Non-starchy vegetables can also help you lose weight by reducing your appetite because they are loaded with fiber.

Here is a short list of some of the best vegetables to eat on the ketogenic diet:

Lettuce

Lettuce is the best vegetable for a ketogenic lifestyle. Lettuce contains few carbohydrates and is a great source of potassium, protein, fiber, and energy. Lettuce also contains many beneficial minerals and vitamins including iron, magnesium, calcium, phosphorus, sodium, niacin, folate, vitamin B6, vitamin A, and vitamin K. Lettuce can also be a healthy ketogenic alternative for hamburger buns and taco shells.

Broccoli

Broccoli is healthy and delicious and rich in nutrients, fiber, calcium, protein, and potassium.

Spinach

Spinach is one of the best vegetables rich in potassium, proteins, and iron. Spinach is also delicious and can be used for salads, stuffing, side dishes, and much more.

Cauliflower

Cauliflower is an excellent source of choline, dietary fiber, omega-3 fatty acids, phosphorus, biotin, vitamins B1, B2, and B3. You can use cauliflower to prepare rice, pizza crusts, hummus, and breadsticks.

Tomatoes

Tomatoes carry many positive health benefits and are a great source of vitamin A, C, and K. Including these vitamins, tomatoes are high in potassium, which can reduce blood pressure levels and decrease stroke risks. When you roast tomatoes with olive oil, you can enhance the lycopene content, boosting its effects. It can also protect heart health and reduce the risk of cancer.

Avocados

Avocados are rich in omega oils. Avocados can be consumed in salads or mixed with other ingredients such as yogurt and nuts. They are high in potassium and fiber and are great for your metabolism and heart. Most grocery stores will sell them in a semi-ripened condition, so you can keep them for up to a week as they ripen. Avocados also have high oil content and minerals, which reduce your appetite and provide nutrients all around for your body.

Asparagus

Asparagus is a great source of minerals and vitamins, including vitamin A, C, and K. Studies have shown that asparagus can help cope with anxiety and protect mental health. Consider eating roasted asparagus for dinner or add raw asparagus in your salads.

Mushrooms

Mushrooms contain strong anti-inflammatory properties, which can improve inflammation for those who have metabolic problems. Mushrooms are also packed with copper, potassium, protein, and selenium. It is also a great source of phosphorus, niacin, pantothenic acid, and zinc, especially if you cook them until brown.

Zucchini

Zucchini is low-carb vegetable and a great source of vitamin A, magnesium, potassium, copper, phosphorus, and folate. Zucchini is also high in omega-3 fatty acids, protein, zinc, and niacin. If you include zucchini in your diet, it can lead to an optimal healthy lifestyle.

Bell Peppers

Bell peppers are nutritious and packed with fiber and vitamins. Bell peppers also contain anti-inflammatory properties that are useful on the ketogenic diet.

Proteins

Following a ketogenic diet requires you to find a source of protein. Proteins consist of amino acids, which are essential nutrients for your body and brain. You need to consume protein, as it is your primary fuel source on this diet. Here are some things you might consider adding to your plate:

Meat and Poultry

Any kind of meat can be used for the ketogenic diet, especially if they are high in fat. Always choose meat from grass-fed and wild animal sources. Avoid hot dogs and sausages, and meat covered with starch or processed sauces.

Fish

Fish is another great source of protein. As with meat and poultry, always choose organic and wild fish caught naturally. Examples of good fish include salmon, trout, tuna, shrimp, cod, lobster, and catfish.

Eggs

Eggs are an incredible source of protein and contain low carbs, especially the egg yolk.

Fats and Oils

Since you will need to burn fat for energy, include fats and oils in your diet. Instead of vegetable oil, go for olive oil, coconut oil, avocado oil, and ghee.

Also, buy oils that are rich in polyunsaturated fats and have a low smoke level; these oils will retain their fatty acids. Such oils include walnut oil, flax oil, hemp seed oil, and grape seed oil.

Dairy Products

For a ketogenic diet, consider consuming raw and organic dairy products. You can use cheeses and creams to prepare ketogenic meals. Examples of the best dairy products to include in your diet are mozzarella cheese, cheddar cheese, parmesan cheese, cottage cheese, sour cream, cream cheese, heavy whipping cream, and Greek yogurt.

Nuts and Seeds

Nuts contain healthy fats and nutrients such as vitamin E. When choosing nuts, purchase roasted nuts because they already have their anti-nutrients discarded. Best nuts and seeds for this diet include walnuts, almonds, and macadamias. They are low in calories and can help you control your carbohydrate count. You can also use products such as almond flour as an alternative to regular flour.

Fruits

You can eat fruits on the keto diet but keep in moderation. Some fruits retract you from reaching ketosis. Berries though, are the most advantageous as they are packed with nutrition and hold a low level in sugar.

What Foods Should not be on Your Plate?

To reach ketosis successfully, do your best to prevent and rid your body of foods that will hold you back from your goal. Most foods to avoid are high in carbohydrates and do not allow your body to burn fat for energy. Here is a general list of the types of foods to avoid:

Root Vegetables

Vegetables that grow and get pulled from the ground are high in carbohydrates and take you away from ketosis. Such vegetables include potatoes, beets, radishes, carrots, onions, and parsnips.

Sweet Fruits

While following the ketogenic diet you should avoid most fruits. Fruits contain fructose (similar to glucose), and is bad for reaching ketosis. Not only avoid fruits; stay away from products made with fresh fruit, such as juices and extracts. If you eat fruits, then keep it in moderation.

Grains

Obviously, avoid all foods made with processed grains. Grains contain additives that can negatively affect your insulin levels. Such grains include bread, pasta, cakes, breadcrumbs, cookies, and pastries.

Diet Soda

Diet soda claims to not contain sugars or carbs; it contains artificial sweeteners equally as detrimental as regular sugar. Artificial sweeteners enhance your carbohydrate intake and prevent you from reaching the metabolic state of ketosis.

Alcohol

Most alcohol beverages consist of none, or low carbs, but can still be bad for a keto lifestyle. Alcohol prevents the fat burning process or dramatically slows it down, because your body will need to process the alcohol first before the fat. To be successful with this diet, limit your alcohol intake.

Processed Foods

Avoid processed or packaged foods. Such foods are packed with artificial additives that can stray you from ketosis. Instead of choosing the processed foods, pick organic and real ingredients.

This is all you need to know about the ketogenic diet. Opinions differ between some individuals and sources, but you get the concept. The ketogenic diet and instant pot have plenty lot in common. It can be used together make fast, tasty, and healthy dishes that will improve your life. Since the keto diet asks you to avoid greasy foods, the instant pot helps by softening up foods using pressure and heat. With that being said, let's use the instant pot to prepare ketogenic meals for better health.

Chapter 2: All About The Slow Cooker

What is a Slow Cooker?

A slow cooker is also known as a crock pot. It is a countertop electrical appliance that simmers food at a lower temperature than cooking methods such as frying, boiling and baking. This enables cooking to be left unattended for many hours without worrying about the food overcooking or burning.

How to Use a Slow Cooker Properly

1. Make sure the temperature is set correctly. If you need to cook something quickly, set the temperature on high.

2. Place the slow cooker on a sturdy surface; it also helps if you set it on top of a tea towel to soak up any liquid that might spit or spill out of it.

3. Don't rest your slow cooker against a wall or too close to any other appliances because of the amount of heat that it produces.

4. Remove any leftovers from the cooker and transfer them into a container. Allow them to cool down before placing them in the refrigerator. Don't let food cool down in the slow cooker because it retains heat for a long time; while it's cooling, bacteria can build up.

5. Don't lift the lid up to check on your food. The heat lost will extend the cooking time for approximately 20 to 30 minutes.

What Are the Benefits of Using a Slow Cooker?

Easy and Quick: Slow cookers make cooking a healthy meal simple. All you have to do is put the ingredients into the slow cooker, set the timer and the temperature setting, and then wait for your meal to cook.

Saves money: A slow cooker doesn't use as much electricity as a regular electric stove, which not only saves money but is also good for the environment.

Healthy: Slow cookers often don't require you to use any fats or oils during the cooking process, so they cook healthier meals. A lot of the vitamins, nutrients and minerals are preserved because foods cook in their own juices.

Flavor: Without you putting in a lot of effort, slow cookers produce more flavor than regular cooking. The food is left to cook for hours, and so the full flavor of sauces become richer as the flavor is released. The food is not cooked with a regular lid, but it is sealed onto the cooker and so there is no loss of flavor through evaporation.

Saves time: The only requirement of using a slow cooker is that you add all the ingredients in together; therefore it saves you time. You only need to use one kitchen utensil, so it also saves time cleaning up.

No burnt food: The food is cooked at a low temperature, so there is no chance of it getting burnt or sticking to the bottom of the pan.

Keeps the kitchen cool: A regular oven and stove not only cooks your food, it also cooks your kitchen! You don't have this problem with a slow cooker.

Tips for Using a Slow Cooker

- When using ingredients such as pasta, rice and fresh herbs, add them towards the end during the final 30 to 60 minutes.

- If you want your sauces to thicken, add flour or corn starch.

- Don't put too many ingredients in your slow cooker; fill it between one half and two thirds full.

- Trim any excess fats from meat; this will make your gravies and sauces silkier.

- If you are using wine among your ingredients, you only need to use a splash; alcohol doesn't evaporate because the cooker is sealed.

Using a Slow Cooker do's and Don'ts

- **Do** brown your meat before placing it into the slow cooker to make sure that it reaches the temperature standards for food safety.

- **Do** wash the insert of your slow cooker with hot soapy water before using it.

- **Do** thaw frozen foods before adding them to the slow cooker. If you don't, it will increase the cooking time.

- **Do** spray the cooker insert with a non-stick cooking spray before you put any food in it. This will make cleanup a lot easier.

- **Do** add tender ingredients such as mushrooms, fish, zucchini and peas during the final 30 minutes to 1 hour of cooking. This will enable them to release their flavors without getting mushy because they have been over cooked.

- **Do** arrange the foods that take longer to cook at the bottom of the cooker.

- **Don't** use abrasive cleansers and sponges to clean the cooker insert or it will get scratched and damaged.

- **Don't** reheat meat leftovers in a slow cooker; the temperature won't get hot enough to heat the food to meat safety standards. Instead, use a microwave.

- **Don't** store leftovers in the slow cooker; transfer them into a container and store them in the fridge.

- **Don't** place the cooker insert over direct heat such as an electric or a gas burner; extreme or sudden temperature changes can cause it to break. For the same reason, **don't** put the insert in the freezer or the oven.

- **Don't** add dairy products until the final thirty minutes to one hour of cooking; when they are cooked too long on a high temperature, dairy products start curdling and separating.

- **Don't** preheat your slow cooker unless the recipe you are making requires you to.

- **Don't** place your slow cooker next to a draft or near an open window; this will cause the slow cooker not to reach its maximum temperature.

- **Don't** open the lid and stir your ingredients. Stirring isn't necessary because one of the advantages of using a slow cooker is that it prevents the food from sticking to the bottom.

Maintenance of a Slow Cooker

- Soak your slow cooker insert in soapy water for 2 hours before washing it. Make sure the tap water is at its hottest temperature.

- If you are still finding your slow cooker difficult to clean after soaking it for 2 hours, sprinkle ¼ cup of baking soda into the slow cooker, add some dish soap, fill it with water and turn it on high for 2 to 4 hours.

- When you are cooking with foods that burn easily. such as sugar and BBQ sauce. use a crock pot liner.

- Make sure your slow cooker is turned off when it is not in use.

- Do not use the glass lid or stoneware liner if it is severely scratched, chipped or cracked.

- For the removal of mineral deposits or water spots, use distilled white vinegar to wipe the liner down.

- Use a soft slightly damp sponge or cloth to wipe the exterior and the interior base.

Chapter 3: Ketogenic Slow Cooker Recipes

Delicious Breakfast Recipes

Tasty Sausage & Eggplant Bake
(Preparation time: 4 hours/Serves 4 people)

Ingredients

- 2 cups of cubed eggplant, salted and drained
- 1 tablespoon of olive oil
- 2 pounds of spicy pork sausage
- 1 tablespoon of Worcestershire sauce
- 1 tablespoon of mustard
- 2 cans of Italian diced tomatoes
- 1 jar of tomato paste
- 2 cups of shredded mozzarella cheese

Directions

1. Use the olive oil to grease the crock pot.
2. In a large bowl, combine the sausage, mustard and Worcestershire sauce and tomato paste; then add   to the crock pot.
3. Add the eggplant on top of the sausage mixture.
4. Pour the tomatoes on top of the mixture; sprinkle the cheese over the top.
5. Cook the ingredients for 4 hours on low.

Nutritional Value

- Carbohydrates: 6 grams
- Protein: 15 grams
- Calories: 210 grams
- Fat: 12 grams

Amazing Artichoke Hearts Bake

Preparation time: 4-6 hours/Serves:4 servings)

Ingredients

- 8 large eggs
- ¾ cup of unsweetened silk almond milk
- 5 ounces of fresh chopped spinach
- 6 ounces of chopped artichoke hearts
- 1 cup of grated Parmesan cheese
- 3 minced cloves of garlic
- 1 teaspoon of salt
- ¾ cup of coconut flour
- 1 tablespoon of baking powder
- 1 tablespoon of olive oil

Directions

1. In a large bowl, whisk together all of the ingredients.
2. Grease the slow cooker with olive oil.
3. Pour the ingredients into the slow cooker, cover and cook for 4-6 hours.

Nutritional Value

- Calories: 141
- Fat: 7.1 grams
- Carbohydrates: 3.8 grams
- Fiber: 4 grams
- Protein: 10 grams

Sweet Ham Maple Breakfast

(Preparation time:3-4 hours/Serves:4 servings -- with leftovers)

Ingredients

- 3-poun fully-cooked boneless ham
- ½ cup of maple syrup
- ½ cup of Honey Dijon Mustard
- ½ cup of packed brown sugar

Directions

1. Make cross shaped diagonal patterns on the ham with a knife and place it into a slow cooker.
2. In a large bowl, whisk together the rest of the ingredients and pour over the ham.
3. Cover and cook on low for 3-4 hours.
4. Take the ham out and cover with foil for 10 minutes.
5. Slice and serve.

Nutritional Value

- Calories: 430
- Fat: 24 grams
- Fiber: 0 grams
- Protein: 32 grams
- Carbohydrates: 13 grams

Lovely Sausage Casserole Breakfast

(Preparation time: 4-5 hours/Serves: 4 servings)

Ingredients

- 8 large eggs
- 1 ½ cups of low fat milk
- 1 pound of cooked bulk sausage, drained
- 1 seeded and chopped jalapeño
- 1 chopped red bell pepper
- ¾ cup sliced green onions
- 2 cups of low fat Mexican blend cheese
- 9 corn tortillas
- ½ cup of salsa

Directions

1. In a large bowl, whisk together the eggs, jalapeño and milk.
2. In another large bowl combine the cheese, green onions, sausage and red bell pepper.
3. Arrange 3 tortillas on the base of a greased slow cooker.
4. Spread a layer of the sausage mixture over the tortillas.
5. Repeat the layering and then pour the egg mixture over the top.
6. Cover and cook on low for 4-5 hours.
7. Divide onto plates and serve with the salsa.

Nutritional Value

- Calories: 386
- Fat: 24 grams
- Fiber: 2.6 grams
- Protein: 24.7 grams

Wonderful Avocado Egg Breakfast

(Preparation time: 45 minutes/Serves: 4 servings)

Ingredients

- 2 large eggs
- 1 large avocado
- Black pepper

Directions

1. Pre-heat the slow cooker on high. Arrange a sheet of baking paper on the bottom of the cooker.
2. Slice the avocado in half, remove the seed and place the avocado on the baking paper, seed-hollowed side up.
3. Crack one egg into each of the avocado holes and sprinkle with black pepper.
4. Cover and cook on high for 45 minutes.
5. Remove and serve.

Nutritional Values

- Calories: 268
- Fat: 12.4 grams
- Protein: 7.5 grams
- Carbohydrates: 9 grams
- Dietary Fiber: 6.7 grams

Beautiful Mushroom Bacon Breakfast

(Preparation time: 4-6 hours/Serving: 4 servings)

Ingredients

- 2 cups of ground sausage, cooked
- ½ cup of chopped onion
- 1 tablespoon of dried parsley
- 1 teaspoon of garlic powder
- 1 teaspoon of thyme
- 6 slices of bacon, cooked and crumbled
- 2 cups of organic chicken broth
- 1 red bell pepper, chopped
- ½ cup of parmesan cheese
- 1 cup of heavy cream
- 2 cups of sliced mushrooms
- Salt and black pepper

Directions

1. Place all of the ingredients into a large slow cooker.
2. Cook for 4-6 hours on a low setting.
3. Make sure that you don't overcook the ingredients or cook the food at a heat that is too high. This will cause the cream to separate.
4. When the food is cooked, divide onto plates and serve hot.

Nutritional Value

- Carbohydrates: 2.1 grams
- Fat: 15.5 grams
- Calories: 166 calories
- Fiber: 0.3 grams
- Protein: 6.7 grams

Delicious Zucchini Cinnamon Nut Bread

(Preparation time:3 hours/Serves: 4 people)

Ingredients

- 2 cups of zucchini, shredded
- ½ cup of ground walnuts
- 1 cup of ground almonds
- 1/3 cup of coconut flakes
- 2 teaspoons of cinnamon
- ½ teaspoon of baking soda
- 1 ½ teaspoons of baking powder
- ½ teaspoon of salt
- 3 large eggs
- 1/3 cup of softened coconut oil
- 1 cup of sweetener of your choice
- 2 teaspoons of vanilla

Directions

1. In a large bowl, beat the vanilla, sweetener, oil and eggs and whisk them together thoroughly.
2. Add all of the dry ingredients to the egg mixture.
3. Add the walnuts and the zucchini.
4. You will need a bread pan that is small enough to fit into the crock pot. Pour the batter into it.
5. Roll up aluminium foil into four balls and set them on the base of the crock pot.
6. Place the pan into the crock pot and place a paper towel over the top to absorb condensation.
7. Place a lid on the slow cooker and cook for 3 hours on high.
8. Allow the bread to cool down, wrap it in foil and place it in the fridge.
9. Serve cold with coffee or tea.

Nutritional Values

- Carbohydrates: 4 grams
- Protein: 5 grams
- Fat: 18 grams
- Calories: 210 grams

Mouth-Watering Cauliflower & Cheese Bake

(Preparation time:4 hours/Serves: 4 people)

Ingredients

- 1 cauliflower head cut into florets
- ½ cup of cream cheese
- ¼ cup of whipping cream
- 3 tablespoons of butter or lard, divided
- 1 teaspoon of salt
- ½ teaspoon of ground black pepper
- ½ cup of shredded cheddar cheese
- 6 slices of crispy bacon, crumbled

Directions

1. Use 1 tablespoon of butter or lard to grease the crock-pot.
2. Add the remaining ingredients to the crock-pot except the bacon and cheddar cheese.
3. Cook for 3 hours on low.
4. Remove the lid and add the cheddar cheese. Cover and cook for another hour.
5. Sprinkle the bacon over the top. Divide onto plates and serve.

Nutritional Value

- Carbohydrates: 3 grams
- Protein: 11 grams
- Fat: 20 grams
- Calories: 232

Spectacular Ham and Spinach Frittata

(Preparation time: 2 hours/Serves: 4 people)

Ingredients

- 10 large eggs
- ½ diced green bell pepper, diced
- 1 cup of ham, diced
- 2 handfuls of fresh spinach
- Salt and pepper

Directions

1. Place a liner in the slow cooker and grease it with non-stick cooking spray.
2. Put the peppers, spinach and ham into the slow cooker.
3. Crack the eggs into a large bowl and whisk together thoroughly. Add salt and pepper and then pour the eggs into the slow cooker.
4. Cook the ingredients on high for 1 ½ to 2 hours.
5. Slice the frittata, divide onto plates and serve.

Nutritional Value

- Calories: 109
- Fat: 6.9 grams
- Carbohydrates: 1.8 grams
- Fiber: 1 gram
- Protein: 5.6 grams

Flavorful Lunch Recipes

Amazing Sour Cream Chicken

(Preparation time:6 hours/Serves: 4 servings)

Ingredients

- 1 cup of sour cream
- ½ cup of chicken stock
- 1 can of diced green chillies and tomatoes
- 1 batch of taco seasoning
- 2 pounds of chicken breast

Directions

1. Add all the ingredients to the slow cooker.
2. Cook on low for 6 hours.
3. Divide onto plates and serve.

Nutritional Value

- Calories: 262
- Fat: 13 grams
- Fiber: 2.5 grams
- Protein: 32 grams
- Carbohydrates: 23 grams

Mouth Watering Minced Pork Zucchini Lasagne

(Preparation time: 8 hours/Serves: 4 servings)

Ingredients

- 4 medium zucchinis
- 1 diced small onion
- 1 minced clove of garlic
- 2 cups of minced lean ground pork
- 2 cans of Italian diced tomatoes
- 2 tablespoons of olive oil
- 2 cups of shredded Mozzarella cheese
- 1 large egg
- 1 tablespoon of dried basil
- Salt and pepper
- 2 tablespoons of butter

Directions

1. Slice the zucchini lengthwise into 6 slices.
2. Heat the olive oil in a saucepan, and sauté the garlic and onions for 5 minutes.
3. Add the minced meat and cook for a further 5 minutes.
4. Add the tomatoes and cook for a further 5 minutes.
5. Add the seasoning and mix together thoroughly.
6. In a small bowl, combine the egg and cheese and whisk together.
7. Use the butter to grease the crock pot and then begin to layer the lasagne.
8. First layer with the zucchini slices, add the meat mixture and then top with the cheese.
9. Repeat and finish with the cheese.
10. Cover and cook for 8 hours on low.

Nutritional Values

- Carbohydrates: 10 grams
- Protein: 23 grams
- Fat: 30 grams
- Calories: 398

Fantastic Lemon Thyme Chicken

(Preparation time: 4 hours/Serves: 4 servings)

Ingredients

- 10-15 cloves of garlic
- 2 sliced lemons
- ½ teaspoon of ground pepper
- 1 teaspoon of thyme
- 3 ½-pound whole chicken

Directions

1. Arrange the lemon and garlic on the base of a slow cooker.
2. Mix the spices together and use them to season the chicken.
3. Put the chicken in the slow cooker.
4. Cover and cook on low for 4 hours.
5. Remove the chicken, let it stand for 15 minutes and then serve.

Nutrition Values

- Calories: 120
- Fat: 8 grams
- Carbohydrates: 1 gram
- Fiber: 0 grams
- Protein: 12 grams

Beautiful BBQ Ribs

(Preparation time: 8 hours/Serves:4 servings)

Ingredients

- 3 pounds of pork ribs
- 1 tablespoon of olive oil
- 1 can of tomato paste, 28 ounces
- ½ cup of hot water
- ½ cup of vinegar
- 6 tablespoons of Worcestershire sauce
- 4 tablespoons of dry mustard
- 1 tablespoon of chili powder
- 1 teaspoon of ground cumin
- 1 teaspoon of powdered sweetener of your choice
- Salt and pepper

Directions

1. Heat the olive oil in a large frying pan and brown the ribs.
2. Place them in the crock pot.
3. In a small bowl, combine the remainder of the ingredients, whisk together thoroughly and pour over the ribs.
4. Cook for 8 hours on low.

Nutritional Value

- Carbohydrates: 14 grams
- Protein: 38 grams
- Fat: 28 grams
- Calories: 410

Delightful Balsamic Oregano Chicken

(Preparation time:4 hours/Serves: 6 people)

Ingredients

- 6 pieces of boneless, skinless chicken
- 2 cans of diced tomatoes, 14.5 ounces
- 1 large onion, thinly sliced
- 4 cloves of garlic
- ½ cup of balsamic vinegar
- 1 tablespoon of olive oil
- 1 tablespoon of dried oregano
- 1 teaspoon of dried rosemary
- 1 teaspoon of dried basil
- ½ teaspoon of thyme
- Salt and pepper

Directions

1. In a small bowl combine all the ingredients except the chicken. Mix them together thoroughly.
2. Place the chicken in the slow cooker and pour the remaining ingredients over the top.
3. Cover and cook on high for 4 hours.

Nutritional Value

- Calories: 190
- Fat: 6 grams
- Carbohydrates: 5 grams
- Fiber: 1 gram
- Protein: 26 grams

Scrumptious Bay Leaf Pork Roast Shoulder

(Preparation time: 8 hours/Serves: 4 servings)

Ingredients

- 3 pounds of whole pork shoulder
- 1 can of Italian diced tomatoes
- 1 diced sweet onion
- 3 diced cloves of garlic
- 4 tablespoons of lard
- 1 cup of water
- 1 bay leaf
- ¼ teaspoon of ground cloves
- Salt and pepper

Directions

1. Place all the ingredients in the crock pot.
2. Cover and cook for 8 hours on low.

Nutritional Values

- Carbohydrates: 10 grams
- Protein: 33 grams
- Fat: 30 grams
- Calories: 421

Tantalizing Chicken Breast with Artichoke Stuffing

(Preparation time: 4 hours/Serves: 4 servings)

Ingredients

- 4 boneless, skinless chicken breasts
- 3 cups of finely chopped spinach
- ½ cup of chopped roasted red peppers
- ¼ cup of sliced black olives
- 1 cup of chopped canned artichoke hearts
- 4 ounces of reduced fat feta cheese
- 1 teaspoon of dried oregano
- 1 teaspoon of garlic powder
- 1 ½ cups of low-sodium chicken broth
- Salt and pepper

Directions

1. Make a deep cut in the center of the chicken and season it with salt and pepper.
2. In a small bowl combine the garlic, feta, oregano, peppers, spinach, and artichoke hearts.
3. Stuff the artichoke mixture into the cut in the chicken and put it into the slow cooker.
4. Cover and cook on low for 4 hours.

Nutritional Values

- Calories: 222
- Fat: 7 grams
- Carbohydrates: 4 grams
- Fiber: 0 grams
- Protein: 52 grams

Gorgeous Coconut Turmeric Pork Curry
(Preparation time:8 hours/Serves: 4 people)

Ingredients

- 2.2 pounds of cubed pork shoulder
- 1 tablespoon of coconut oil
- 1 tablespoon of olive oil
- 1 diced yellow onion
- 2 cloves of minced garlic
- 2 tablespoons of tomato paste
- 1 can of coconut milk, 12 ounces
- 1 cup of water
- ½ cup of white wine
- 1 teaspoon of turmeric
- 1 teaspoon of ginger powder
- 1 teaspoon of curry powder
- ½ teaspoon of paprika
- Salt and pepper

Directions

1. Heat 1 tablespoon of olive oil in a saucepan and sauté the garlic and onions for 3 minutes.
2. Add the pork and brown it, and then add the tomato paste.
3. Mix the remaining ingredients in the crock pot and then add the pork.
4. Cover and cook for 8 hours on low.
5. Divide onto plates and serve

Nutritional Value

- Carbohydrates: 7 grams
- Protein: 30 grams
- Fat: 31 grams
- Calories: 425 grams

Tantalizing Pork Chops with Cumin Butter and Garlic

(Preparation time: 3-4 hours/Serves:4 servings)

Ingredients

- 3.5 pounds of pork sirloin chops with the bone
- ½ cup of salsa
- 3 tablespoons of butter
- 5 tablespoons of lime juice
- ½ teaspoon of ground cumin
- ¾ teaspoon of garlic powder
- ¾ teaspoon of salt
- ¾ teaspoon of black pepper

Directions

1. Combine the spices and season the pork chops.
2. Melt the butter in a saucepan and brown the pork chops for 3 minutes on each side.
3. Place the chops into the slow cooker and pour the salsa over the top.
4. Cover and cook on high for 3-4 hours.
5. Divide onto plates and serve.

Nutritional Value

- Calories: 364
- Fat: 17 grams
- Carbohydrates: 3 grams
- Fiber: 0 grams
- Protein: 51 grams

Great Dinner Recipes

Delightful Turkey Basil Meatballs

(Preparation time: 4-5 hours/Serves: 4 servings)

Ingredients

- 1 package of frozen turkey meatballs
- ½ a cup of bottled yellow and red sweet peppers, chopped and drained
- 1/8 teaspoon of crushed red peppers
- 1 cup of reduced sodium pasta sauce
- Snipped fresh basil for garnish

Directions

1. Place all of the ingredients except the basil into the slow cooker.
2. Cover and cook on low for 4-5 hours.
3. Divide onto plates, garnish with the basil and serve.

Nutritional Values

- Calories: 68
- Fat: 4 grams
- Carbohydrates: 3 grams
- Protein: 6 grams

Wonderful Weekend Chicken Cooked with Beer

(Preparation time: 6-8 hours/Serves: 4 servings)

Ingredients

- 1 ½ pounds of skinless, boneless chicken breasts
- 1 can of light beer, 12 ounces
- ½ teaspoon of salt
- ½ teaspoon of black pepper
- ½ teaspoon of red pepper flakes
- ½ tablespoon of dried oregano

Directions

1. Using the oregano, salt, black pepper, and red pepper flakes season the chicken and arrange it inside the slow cooker.
2. Pour the beer onto the chicken.
3. Cover and cook on low for 6-8 hours.
4. Use two forks to shred the chicken, divide onto plates and serve.

Nutrition Values

- Calories: 139
- Fat: 3 grams
- Carbohydrates: 0 grams
- Protein: 28 grams

Beautiful Italian Black Olive Chicken

(Preparation time: 6 hours/Serves: 4 servings)

Ingredients

- 2 pounds of skinless, boneless chicken breasts
- 1 teaspoon of Italian seasoning
- Salt and pepper
- ½ teaspoon of basil
- ¼ teaspoon of red pepper flakes
- 35 pieces of turkey pepperoni, cut in half
- ½ cup of reduced sodium black olives

Directions

1. Use the salt and pepper to season the chicken and arrange it in the slow cooker.
2. Add the pepperoni and the olives.
3. Whisk the remaining ingredients together and pour on top of the chicken.
4. Cover and cook on low for 6 hours.
5. Shred the chicken, divide onto plates and serve.

Nutritional Value

- Calories: 307
- Fat: 10 grams
- Carbohydrates: 4 grams
- Protein: 52 grams

Spectacular One Pot Special Meal
(Preparation time: 5 hours/Serves: 4 servings)

Ingredients

- 1 chopped green bell pepper
- 1 cup of fresh spinach
- 1 diced red onion
- 2 cloves of minced garlic
- 1 can of Italian tomatoes, diced
- 2 cups of chicken broth
- 2 tablespoons of tomato paste
- 1 cup of sliced black olives
- 1 cup of dry white wine
- 2 bay leaves
- 1 teaspoon of dry basil
- ¼ teaspoon of crushed fennel seeds
- 1 ¾ cups of peeled shrimp, medium size
- 1 ¾ cups of cod, cubed
- Salt and pepper

Directions

1. Add all of the ingredients except the cod and the shrimp to the crock pot.
2. Cover and cook for 4.5 hours on low.
3. Add the cod and the shrimp, cover and cook for a further 30 minutes.

Nutritional Value

- Carbohydrates: 9 grams
- Protein: 36 grams
- Fat: 25 grams
- Calories: 436 grams

Cinnamon, Coriander, Broccoli Oxtail Pot

(Preparation time: 8-10 hours/Serves: 4 servings)

Ingredients

- 3 pounds of oxtail cut into small chunks
- 2 tablespoons of olive oil
- 1 diced red onion
- 3 cloves of minced garlic
- A chunk of fresh ginger, peeled and sliced thinly
- 1 can of diced Italian tomatoes
- 1 teaspoon of ground cardamom
- 1 teaspoon of ground cumin
- 1 teaspoon of ground coriander seeds
- ½ teaspoon of cinnamon
- 1 ½ teaspoons of salt
- 1 teaspoon of fresh ground pepper
- 1 cup of hot water and 1 cup of beef broth
- 5 cubed small turnips
- 1 chopped head of broccoli
- 1 cup of diced mushrooms

Directions

1. Preheat the slow cooker on low.
2. Heat the olive oil in a pan, brown the oxtail and add it to the crock pot.
3. Sauté the onions in the same pan for 5 minutes. When they become translucent, add the ginger and the garlic, cook for a further 1 minute. Once cooked, pour these over the oxtail.
4. Add the rest of the ingredients to the saucepan and allow them to boil.
5. Pour the sauce into the slow cooker and stir; the liquid should cover the oxtail. If you need to, add some more water.
6. Cover and cook for 8-10 hours on low.

Nutritional Values

- Carbohydrates: 14 grams
- Protein: 68 grams
- Fat: 31 grams
- Calories: 510

Tasty Ham and Cauliflower Stew

(Preparation time:4 hours/Serves: 4 servings)

Ingredients

- 3 cups of diced ham
- 16 ounces of frozen cauliflower florets
- ¼ cup of heavy cream
- 14.5 ounces of chicken broth
- ¼ teaspoon of salt
- 4 cloves of garlic
- 8 ounces of grated cheddar cheese
- ½ teaspoon of garlic powder
- ½ teaspoon of onion powder
- A dash of pepper

Directions

1. Place all the ingredients into the slow cooker.
2. Cook on high for 4 hours.

Nutritional Values

- Calories: 320
- Fat: 20.6 grams
- Carbohydrates: 7.5 grams
- Fiber: 3 grams
- Protein: 23.3 grams

Easy Soup Recipes

Superb Chicken, Bacon, Garlic Thyme Soup
(Preparation time: 6 hours/Serves: 4 servings)

Ingredients

- 2 tablespoons of unsalted butter
- 1 chopped onion
- 1 chopped pepper
- 8 chicken thighs
- 8 slices of bacon
- 1 tablespoon of thyme
- 1 teaspoon of salt
- 1 teaspoon of pepper
- 1 tablespoon of minced garlic
- 1 tablespoon of coconut flour
- 3 tablespoons of lemon juice
- 1 cup of chicken stock
- ¼ cup of unsweetened coconut milk
- 3 tablespoons of tomato paste

Directions

1. Spread the butter on the base of the slow cooker and arrange the peppers and onions on top of it.
2. Add the chicken thighs and then layer with the bacon.
3. Add the remaining ingredients.
4. Cover and cook on low for 6 hours.
5. Cut the thighs into pieces, arrange in bowls and serve.

Nutritional Values

- Calories: 396
- Fat: 21 grams
- Carbohydrates: 7 grams
- Fiber: 2 grams
- Protein: 41 grams

Delightful Chicken-Chorizo Spicy Soup
(Preparation time: 3.5 hours/Serves: 10 servings)

Ingredients

- 4 pounds of skinless, boneless, chicken
- 1 pound of chorizo
- 4 cups of chicken stock
- 1 cup of heavy cream
- 1 can of stewed tomatoes
- 2 tablespoons of minced garlic
- 2 tablespoons of Worcestershire sauce
- 2 tablespoons of red sauce
- Parmesan and sour cream for garnish

Directions

1. Heat a frying pan and brown the sausage.
2. Place the chicken into the slow cooker and add the remaining ingredients except the Parmesan and sour cream.
3. Cover and cook on high for 3 hours.
4. Garnish with the Parmesan and the sour cream.

Nutritional Value

- Calories: 659
- Fat: 37 grams
- Carbohydrates: 6 grams
- Fiber: 1 gram
- Protein: 52 grams

Delectable Spearmint Liver and Lamb Heart Soup

(Preparation time: 10 hours/Serves: 4 people)

Ingredients

- 3 cups of livers and lamb hearts
- 1 cup of cubed lamb meat
- 2 cups of broth of your choice
- 2 cups of hot water
- 2 bunches of diced spring onions
- 1 bunch of chopped fresh spearmint
- 2 cups of fresh spinach
- 1 teaspoon of garlic powder
- 1 teaspoon of dried basil
- 1 teaspoon of sweet paprika
- 1 teaspoon of ground pimento
- 4 lightly crushed cloves
- ½ teaspoon of cinnamon
- 4 tablespoons of olive oil
- Salt and pepper
- 1 large egg
- 1 cup of Greek yogurt, full fat

Directions

1. Add all of the ingredients to the slow cooker except the yogurt and the egg.
2. Cover and cook for 10 hours on low.
3. Remove the meat, cut into bite sized chunks, and return to the crock pot.
4. In a small bowl whisk together the yogurt and the egg. Add some of the cooked liquid from the slow cooker. Mix together thoroughly.
5. Pour the mixture into the slow cooker and stir to combine.
6. Allow to heat through, and serve.

Nutritional Value

- Carbohydrates: 12 grams
- Protein: 56 grams
- Fat: 38 grams
- Calories: 560

Lovely Lentil Sausage Soup

(Preparation time:6-8 hours/Serves:4 servings)

Ingredients

- 1 ½ pounds of Italian sausage
- 2 tablespoons of butter
- 2 tablespoons of olive oil
- 5 cups of chicken stock
- 1 ½ cups of lentils
- 1 cup of spinach
- ½ cup of diced carrots
- 4 minced cloves of garlic
- 1 trimmed leek
- 1 diced celery rib
- 1 cup of heavy cream
- ½ cup of shredded Parmesan cheese
- 2 tablespoons of Dijon mustard
- 2 tablespoons of red wine vinegar
- Salt and pepper

Directions

1. Place the stock and the lentils into the slow cooker.
2. In a saucepan, heat the olive oil and the butter and brown the sausage.
3. In the same saucepan, sauté the celery, pepper, salt, garlic, leek, spinach, onions and carrots for 10 minutes.
4. Pour the mixture into the slow cooker.
5. Cook on low for 6-8 hours.
6. Spoon into bowls and serve.

Nutrition Values

- Calories: 195
- Fat: 14 grams
- Carbohydrates: 4.9 grams
- Protein: 11 grams

Tasty Corned Beef and Heavy Cream Soup

(Preparation time:5.5 hours/Serves: 4 servings)

Ingredients

- 1 diced onion
- 2 diced celery ribs
- 2 cloves of minced garlic
- 1 pound of chopped corn beef
- 4 cups of beef stock
- 1 cup of sauerkraut
- 1 teaspoon of sea salt
- 1 teaspoon of caraway seeds
- ¾ teaspoon of black pepper
- 2 cups of heavy cream
- 1 ½ cups of shredded Swiss cheese

Directions

1. Heat the butter in a saucepan and sauté the celery, garlic and onions.
2. Pour the mixture into the slow cooker.
3. Add the remaining ingredients except the cream and the cheese.
4. Cover and cook on low for 4.5 hours.
5. Add the cream and the cheese and cook for another hour.

Nutritional Value

- Calories: 225
- Fat: 18.5 grams
- Carbohydrates: 4 grams
- Protein: 11.5 grams

Delicious Beef Meatball and Sour Cream Soup

(Preparation time: 6 hours/Serves: 4 servings)

Ingredients

- 1 diced red bell pepper
- 8-10 halved pearl onions
- 2 cloves of minced garlic
- 2 tablespoons of olive oil
- 3 cups of lean ground beef
- 1 large egg
- 1 teaspoon of dry savoury
- Salt and pepper
- 1 cup of beef broth
- 2 cups of hot water
- 1 cup of sour cream

Directions

1. Preheat the slow cooker on low.
2. Add the oil and vegetables.
3. In a large bowl combine the egg, salt, pepper, dry savoury, and meat. Mix together thoroughly and shape into approximately 30 small meatballs.
4. Boil the broth in a pot, add the meatballs and cook for 2 minutes.
5. Add the broth and the meatballs to the slow cooker.
6. Cover and cook for 6 hours.
7. Take out a spoonful of the broth and add it to the sour cream, mix together thoroughly and then pour it back into the slow cooker. Stir gently, spoon into bowls and serve.

Nutritional Values

- Carbohydrates: 11 grams
- Protein: 27 grams
- Fat: 28 grams
- Calories: 409

Veggie Soup with Minty Balls

(Preparation time:6-8 hours/Serves: 4 servings)

Ingredients

- 3 cups of beef broth
- 1 medium zucchini sliced into sticks
- 2 diced celery sticks
- 1 diced yellow onion
- 5 crushed cloves of garlic
- 1 cubed medium tomato
- 3 cups of ground veal
- ½ cup of Parmesan cheese
- 1 large egg
- ½ cup of chopped fresh mint
- 1 teaspoon of dry oregano
- 1 teaspoon of sweet paprika
- Salt and pepper

Directions

1. Preheat the slow cooker on low.
2. Add the tomato, onion, celery, zucchini and broth.
3. In a large bowl, combine the meat, salt, pepper, seasoning, mint, egg, garlic and cheese. Shape the meat into small approximately 45 small meat balls.
4. Heat the olive oil in a pan, add the meatballs and brown.
5. Place the meatballs in the slow cooker, add one cup of hot water if more liquid is required.
6. Cover and cook for 6-8 hours on low.
7. Spoon into bowls and serve.

Nutritional Values

- Carbohydrates: 11 grams
- Protein: 32 grams
- Fat: 25 grams
- Calories: 395 grams

Chicken Cordon Bleu Soup

(Preparation time: 6 hours/Serves: 4 servings)

Ingredients

- 12 ounces of diced ham
- 1 pound of chicken breast
- 4 ounces of diced onion
- 5 ounces of chopped mushrooms
- 3 tablespoons of minced garlic
- 6 cups of chicken broth
- 2 teaspoons of tarragon
- 3 tablespoons of salted butter
- 1 teaspoon of sea salt
- 1 teaspoon of black pepper
- 1 ½ cups of heavy cream
- ½ cup of sour cream
- ½ cup of grated parmesan cheese
- 4 ounces of Swiss cheese

Directions

1. Place the onion, tarragon, salt, pepper, ham, mushroom, and broth into the slow cooker.
2. Heat the butter in a saucepan and cook the garlic.
3. Add the chicken and sear it.
4. Place the chicken, garlic and the cheese in the slow cooker.
5. Cover and cook on low for six hours.
6. Add cream, and cook for another hour.
7. Spoon into bowls, top with cheese, and serve.

Nutritional Values

- Calories: 178
- Fat: 12 grams
- Carbohydrates: 2.75 grams
- Protein: 16 grams

Ginger Pumpkin Soup

(Preparation time: 4-6 hours/Serves: 4 servings)

Ingredients

- 1 diced onion
- 1 teaspoon of crushed ginger
- 1 teaspoon of crushed garlic
- ½ stick of butter
- 1 pound of pumpkin chunks
- 2 cups of vegetable stock
- 1 2/3 cups of coconut cream
- Salt and pepper

Directions

1. Place all the ingredients into a slow cooker.
2. Cook on high for 4-6 hours.
3. Puree the soup using an immersion blender.
4. Spoon into bowls and serve.

Nutrition Values

- Calories: 234
- Fat: 21.7 grams
- Carbohydrates: 11.4 grams
- Fiber: 1.5 grams
- Protein: 2.3 grams

Mouth-Watering Meat Recipes

Delightful Spicy Beef
(Preparation time: 8-10 hours/Serves: 4 servings)

Ingredients

- 2 pounds of beef chuck on the bone
- 1 can of chopped tomatoes
- 1 can of chipotle sauce
- 1 can of drained diced jalapeño chilies
- 1 chopped onion
- 3 cloves of minced garlic
- 2 tablespoons of chili powder
- 1 tablespoon of honey
- 2 ½ teaspoons of kosher salt
- 1 teaspoon of ground cumin
- 2 cups of beef broth

Directions

1. Put all the ingredients into a slow cooker.
2. Cover and cook on low for 8 to 10 hours until the beef becomes tender.
3. Take the lid off the slow cooker during the last ½ hour to thicken the sauce.
4. Take the beef out and use a fork to shred it and mix into the sauce in the slow cooker.
5. Divide onto plates and serve.

Nutrition Values

- Calories: 261
- Fat: 11 grams
- Fiber: 1.8 grams
- Protein: 30 grams

Tasty Spiced Chili Beef Eye Roast

(Preparation time: 8 hours/Serves: 4 servings)

Ingredients

- 3 pounds of lean ground beef eye roast
- 2 tablespoons of Worcestershire sauce
- 4 tablespoons of fresh lime juice
- 1 ½ cups of diced onions
- 1 cup of diced red bell pepper
- 3 cloves of minced garlic
- 3 minced and seeded Serrano chilies
- Salt and pepper
- ½ cup of beef broth
- 1 cup of canned tomatoes, diced
- ½ teaspoon of dried oregano

Directions

1. Use salt and pepper to season the beef and put it into the slow cooker.
2. In a large bowl, whisk the remaining ingredients together and pour them over the beef.
3. Cook on low for 8 hours.
4. Use 2 forks to shred the beef

Nutrition Values

- Calories: 247
- Fat: 6 grams
- Fiber: 1 gram
- Protein: 40 grams

Spectacular Meaty Crushed Tomato Bolognese

(Preparation time: 6 hours/Serves: 4 people)

Ingredients

- 4 ounces of chopped pancetta
- 1 tablespoon of butter
- 1 white onion, minced
- 2 stalks of celery, minced
- 2 carrots, minced
- 2 pounds of ground beef, 95% lean
- ¼ cup of white wine
- 2 cans of crushed tomatoes
- 3 bay leaves
- Salt and pepper
- ¼ cup of chopped fresh parsley
- ½ cup of half and half

Directions

1. In a deep pan on low heat, sauté the pancetta for 4-5 minutes.
2. Add the carrots, onions, celery and butter and cook for another 5 minutes.
3. Turn the heat up to medium, add the meat and the pepper and sauté until the meat browns.
4. Drain the fat, add the wine and cook for a further 3-4 minutes.
5. Pour the mixture into the slow cooker, add salt and pepper, the tomatoes and bay leaves.
6. Cover and cook on low for 6 hours.
7. Add the half and half and the parsley
8. Pour over pasta and serve.

Nutrition Values

- Calories: 143
- Fat: 7 grams
- Fiber: 1 gram
- Protein: 15 grams

Wonderful Beef & Bacon Meatballs

(Preparation time: 4-6 hours/Serves: 4 servings)

Ingredients

- 2.2 pounds of ground beef
- 2 slices of diced bacon
- 1 quartered onion
- 2 cloves of garlic
- 1 egg
- Salt and pepper
- A handful of herbs of your choice
- 14 ounces of canned chopped tomatoes

Directions

1. Combine the garlic, onion and bacon in a food processor and work until finely chopped.
2. Add the remaining ingredients except the tomatoes and work until the ingredients turn into a smooth paste.
3. Use your hands to mold the ingredients into meatballs and arrange them in a greased slow cooker.
4. Pour the canned tomatoes over the top, cover and cook on high for 4-6 hours.

Nutrition Values

- Calories: 358
- Fat: 22 grams
- Carbohydrates: 5.2 grams
- Fiber: 1 gram

Yummy Cabbage Rolls and Corned Beef

(Preparation time: 6 hours/Serves: 4 servings)

Ingredients

- 3.5 pounds of corned beef
- 1 sliced onion
- 1 lemon
- ¼ cup of coffee
- ¼ cup of white wine
- 1 tablespoon of bacon fat
- 1 tablespoon of brown mustard
- 1 tablespoon of erythritol
- 2 teaspoons of kosher salt
- 2 teaspoons of Worcestershire sauce
- 1 teaspoon of peppercorns
- ¼ teaspoon of allspice
- 1 crushed bay leaf
- 15 Savoy cabbage leaves

Directions

1. Add the liquids, spices and the beef to the slow cooker.
2. Cover and cook for 6 hours on low.
3. Boil a saucepan of water and add the onions and the cabbage, boil for approximately 2-3 minutes or until the cabbage leaves are soft.
4. Pour ice cold water into a bowl and add the cabbage leaves, allow them to soak for 3-4 minutes.
5. Slice the meat and other ingredients onto the cabbage leaves and roll them tightly.
6. Squeeze the lemon over the top and serve.

Nutrition Values

- Calories: 478
- Fat: 25 grams
- Carbohydrates: 3.8 grams
- Protein: 34.2 grams

Delicious One-Pot Oriental Lamb

(Preparation time: 4 hours/Serves: 4 servings)

Ingredients

- 3 cups of boneless lamb, diced
- 2 tablespoons of almond flour
- 2 cups of fresh spinach
- 2 halved small red onions
- 2 cloves of minced garlic
- ¼ cup of diced yellow turnip
- 2 tablespoons of dry sherry
- 2-3 bay leaves
- 1 teaspoon of hot mustard
- ¼ teaspoon of ground nutmeg
- 1 teaspoon of fresh chopped thyme
- 1 teaspoon of fresh chopped rosemary
- 5-6 whole pimentoes
- 1 1/3 cups of your preferred broth
- Salt and pepper
- 8 halved baby zucchinis
- 2 tablespoons of olive oil

Directions

1. Arrange the lamb in the crock pot, pour the almond flour over the top.
2. Add the rest of the ingredients, cover and cook for 4 hours on high.
3. Serve with a salad of your choice.

Nutritional Value

- Carbohydrates: 24 grams
- Protein: 50 grams
- Fat: 37 grams
- Calories: 510

Tasty Beef Thyme Pot Roast

(Preparation time: 7 hours/Serves: 4 servings)

Ingredients

- 3 pounds of beef chuck roast
- 2 tablespoons of olive oil
- 1 red onion sliced into tiny pieces
- 2 cups of hot water
- 1 cup of beef broth
- 2 tablespoons of butter
- 1 teaspoon of dried rosemary
- 1 teaspoon of dried thyme
- Salt and pepper
- 5 small turnips peeled and cut into strips

Directions

1. Heat the olive oil in a frying pan over high heat and brown the meat on both sides for 2 minutes.
2. Place all ingredients except the turnips into the slow cooker.
3. Cover and cook for five hours on low.
4. Add the turnips and cook for a further 2 hours until the turnips soften.
5. Spoon onto dishes and serve with garlic sauce or sour cream.

Nutritional Value

- Carbohydrates: 13 grams
- Protein: 72 grams
- Fat: 26 grams
- Calories: 459 grams

Beautiful Beef Rosemary Brisket

(Preparation time: 12 hours/Serves: 10 servings)

Ingredients

- 6.6 pounds of whole beef brisket
- 2 tablespoons of olive oil
- 2 tablespoons of apple cider vinegar
- 1 teaspoon of dried oregano
- 1 teaspoon of dry thyme
- 1 teaspoon of dried rosemary
- 2 tablespoons of paprika
- 1 teaspoon of cayenne pepper
- 1 tablespoon of salt
- 1 teaspoon of freshly ground black pepper

Directions

1. In a small bowl, combine the dry seasonings, apple cider vinegar and olive oil.
2. Arrange the meat in the slow cooker and coat with the seasoning mixture.
3. Cover and cook for 12 hours on low.
4. Take the brisket out of the liquid and grill for approximately 2-4 minutes.
5. Place foil over the meat and allow it to rest for 1 hour.
6. Slice and serve.

Nutritional Value

- Carbohydrates: 1 gram
- Protein: 70 grams
- Fat: 28 grams
- Calories: 410 grams

Awesome Cabbage Roast with Cumin Onion Beef

(Preparation time: 8 hours/Serves: 4 people)

Ingredients

- 1 quartered red onion
- 2 cloves of minced garlic
- 2 -3 sticks of diced celery
- 4-6 dry pimentoes
- 2 bay leaves
- 5.5 pounds of beef brisket, cut in two pieces
- 1 teaspoon of chili powder
- 1 teaspoon of ground cumin
- 2 cups of beef broth
- 2 cups of hot water
- Salt and pepper
- 1 medium cabbage cut into quarters

Directions

1. Add all ingredients except the cabbage into the slow cooker.
2. Cover and cook for 7 hours on low.
3. Add the cabbage and cook for a further 1 hour.
4. Spoon onto dishes and serve.

Nutritional Value

- Carbohydrates: 8 grams
- Protein: 32 grams
- Fat: 25 grams
- Calories: 399

Healthy Vegetable Recipes

Tasty Tagine Five a Day

(Preparation time: 8 hours/Serves: 6 servings)

Ingredients

- 4 tablespoons of olive oil
- 1 sliced red onion
- 2 cloves of crushed garlic
- 500 grams of aubergine in 1 cm-thick slices, cut lengthways
- 300 grams of quartered ripe tomatoes
- 1 small sliced fennel bulb
- 50 grams of sundried tomatoes
- 1 teaspoon of coriander seeds

Ingredients for the dressing

- 100 grams of feta cheese, and extra for topping
- 50 grams of toasted almond flakes

Directions

- Pour 2 tablespoons of olive oil into the slow cooker and add the crushed garlic and the onions.
- Brush the aubergines with the remaining olive oil and place them on top of the onions and garlic.
- Arrange the sundried tomatoes, fennel slices, and the tomatoes around the aubergines. Season with salt and pepper and pour the coriander seeds over the top. Cook for 6-8 hours on low.
- Place the dressing ingredients into a food processor and work until smooth. Spoon the vegetables onto serving dishes, drizzle the dressing over the top and crumble the feta cheese on top.

Nutritional Value

Calories: 289, Fat: 20 grams, Carbs: 11 grams, Protein: 8 grams

Beautiful Baked Mushrooms with Pesto & Ricotta

(Preparation time: 4-6 hours/Serves: 4 servings)

Ingredients

- 5 tablespoons of olive oil, extra virgin
- 16 large chestnut mushrooms
- A 250-gram tub of ricotta
- 2 tablespoons of pesto
- 2 finely chopped cloves of garlic
- 25 grams of freshly grated parmesan cheese
- 2 tablespoons of fresh, chopped parsley

Directions

1. Trim the mushroom stems level with the caps.
2. In a small bowl combine the garlic, pesto and ricotta, and spoon into the mushroom heads.
3. Place the mushroom caps in a slow cooker and cook on low for 4-6 hours.
4. In the last half-hour, sprinkle the parmesan cheese over the top of the mushrooms.
5. Serve topped with the fresh parsley.

Nutritional Value

- Calories: 400 grams
- Fat: 34 grams
- Carbohydrates: 2 grams
- Fibre: 1 gram
- Protein: 19 grams

Delicious Dal with Crispy Onions

(Preparation time: 6 hours/Serves:4 servings)

Ingredients

- 250 grams of black urid beans
- 100 grams of ghee or butter
- 2 large onions thinly sliced
- 3 cloves of crushed garlic
- 1 piece of ginger, thumb sized and finely chopped
- 2 teaspoons of ground cumin
- 2 teaspoons of ground coriander
- 1 teaspoon of ground turmeric
- 1 teaspoon of paprika
- ¼ teaspoon of chili powder
- A small bunch fresh coriander, reserve the leaves and finely chop the stems
- 400 grams of passata
- 1 red chili, pierced with the tip of a knife
- 50 ml of double cream

Ingredients to serve alongside dal

- Baked sweet potato
- Naan bread
- Cooked rice
- Coriander
- Sliced red chili
- Lime wedges
- Yogurt, cream or swirl
- Indian chutney or pickle
- Crispy salad onions

Directions

1. Soak the beans for 4 hours or overnight in cold water.
2. In a large saucepan, melt the ghee or butter, then add the ginger, onions, and garlic and cook for 15 minutes to caramelize the onions.
3. Add the coriander stems, spices and 100ml of water.
4. Pour the ingredients into the slow cooker and add the chili, passata, beans and 400ml of water. Season and cook for 5-6 hours on low.
5. When cooked, the beans should be tender and the dal should be very thick. Add the cream and serve with a side dish of your choice.

Nutrition Value: Calories: 527, Fat: 34 g, Carbs: 35 g, Protein: 19 g

Delicious Warming Bean and Veg Soup

(Preparation time: 8-10 hours/Serves: 4 servings)

Ingredients

- 2 cloves of minced garlic
- 1 medium sized potato, diced
- 2 carrots, peeled and sliced
- 2 celery stalks, diced
- A handful of frozen broad beans
- 2 tins of butter beans
- Paprika
- Worcestershire sauce
- Chili
- Salt and pepper
- Parmesan cheese
- Fresh herbs of your choice

Directions

1. Add all the ingredients except the Parmesan cheese and the fresh herbs to the slow cooker.
2. Cook on low for 8-10 hours.
3. Spoon onto dishes, top with Parmesan cheese and fresh herbs and serve.

Nutritional Value

- Carbohydrates: 5.2 grams
- Fat: 8 grams
- Protein: 3.7 grams
- Fiber: 7.4 grams
- Calories: 527

Sumptuous Slow-Cooked Baked Beans

(Preparation time: 8 hours/ Serves: 8 servings)

Ingredients

- 1 pound of dried beans of your choice
- 1 diced medium onion
- 1/3 cup of brown sugar
- 1/3 cup of molasses
- ¼ cup of tomato sauce
- 2 tablespoons of yellow mustard
- 1 tablespoon of smoked paprika
- 1 tablespoon of Worcestershire sauce
- 1 tablespoon of cider vinegar or white balsamic vinegar
- Salt and pepper

Directions

1. Rinse the dried beans and pour them into the slow cooker, cover them with 2 inches of water and leave them to soak overnight.
2. The following morning, drain the water from the slow cooker and add the remaining ingredients.
3. Add 2 ½ cups of water and salt and pepper to season.
4. Cook for 8 hours on low.
5. Spoon onto dishes and serve.

Nutritional Value

- Calories: 136
- Fat: 0.2 grams
- Carbohydrates: 30.4 grams
- Fiber: 4.1 grams
- Protein: 3.8 grams

Precious Peppers Stuffed with Black Beans & Quinoa

(Preparation time: Serves: 6 servings)

Ingredients

- 6 bell peppers
- 1 cup of uncooked quinoa
- 1 14-ounce can of black beans, drained and rinsed
- 1 ½ cups of red enchilada sauce
- 1 teaspoon of cumin
- 1 teaspoon of chili powder
- 1 teaspoon of onion powder
- ½ a teaspoon of garlic salt
- 1 ½ cups of Pepperjack cheese, shredded, divided
- Cilantro
- Avocado
- Sour cream

Directions

1. Cut the tops off the peppers and scrape out the insides.
2. Combine 1 cup of cheese, spices, enchilada sauce, beans and quinoa in a large bowl and stir together thoroughly.
3. Stuff the mixture into the peppers.
4. Pour ½ cup of water into the slow cooker.
5. Arrange the peppers in the water.
6. Cover and cook on high low for 6 hours.
7. Take the lid off and sprinkle the peppers with the remaining cheese, cover and cook for a few minutes to melt the cheese.
8. Serve with avocado, sour cream and cilantro.

Nutritional Value

- Calories: 434
- Calories: 116
- Fat: 12.9 grams
- Carbohydrates: 59.5 grams
- Protein: 22.7 grams
- Fiber: 14.4 grams

Tasty Eggplant Parmesan

(Preparation time: 8 hours/Serves: 12 servings)

Ingredients

- 4 pounds of eggplant
- 1 tablespoon of salt
- 3 large eggs
- ¼ cup of milk
- 1 ½ cup of breadcrumbs
- 3 ounces of parmesan cheese
- 2 teaspoons of Italian seasoning
- 4 cups of marinara sauce
- 16 ounces of mozzarella cheese

Directions

1. Peel the eggplant and cut it into 1/3 inch-rounds.
2. Layer the eggplant in a colander and sprinkle each layer with salt. Let sit for 30 minutes and then rinse and pat dry.
3. Spread ½ cup of sauce on the bottom of the slow cooker.
4. In a small bowl, whisk together the milk and eggs.
5. In another small bowl, whisk together the Italian seasoning, Parmesan cheese and breadcrumbs.
6. Dip the eggplant into the egg mixture and then into the breadcrumb mixture.
7. Layer 1/3 of the slices in the slow cooker.
8. Pour 1 cup of sauce and the mozzarella cheese over the top.
9. Repeat twice, cover and cook for 8 hours.
10. Divide onto plates and serve.

Nutrition Facts

- Calories: 258
- Carbohydrates: 23 grams
- Fiber: 6 grams
- Fat: 6 grams
- Protein: 16 grams

Delicious Chili Lentils and Beans

(Preparation time: 8 hours/Serves: 7 servings)

Ingredients

- 1 finely chopped onion
- 3 cloves of minced garlic
- 1 stalk of celery, chopped
- 2 chopped bell peppers
- 1 can of diced tomatoes
- 4 cups of vegetable broth
- 1 can of water
- 1 cup of dried lentils
- 1 can of Bush's Pinto Beans
- 2 tablespoons of chili powder
- 2 teaspoons of cumin
- 1 tablespoon of oregano

Directions

1. Put all of the ingredients into the slow cooker and cook for 8 hours on low.
2. Serve with a combination of the following: cilantro, green onion, avocado, sour cream, plain Greek Yogurt and shredded cheese.

Mouth-watering Butternut Macaroni Squash

(Preparation time: 8 hours/Serves: 5 servings)

Ingredients

- 1 ½ cups of butternut squash, cubed
- ½ cup of chopped tomatoes
- 1 ½ cups of water
- 2 cloves of minced garlic
- A handful of fresh thyme, finely chopped
- A handful of fresh rosemary, finely chopped
- ¼ cup of nutritional yeast
- 1 cup of non-dairy milk
- 1 ½ cups of whole wheat macaroni
- Salt and pepper

Directions

1. Add the butternut squash, chopped tomatoes, water, garlic, thyme, and rosemary to the slow cooker. Cover and cook on low for 7-9 hours.
2. Transfer the ingredients from the slow cooker into a food processor and add the nutritional yeast, half a cup of non-dairy milk and blend.
3. Pour the ingredients back into the slow cooker, add the macaroni, cover and cook for a further 20 minutes on high.
4. Stir, cook for a further 25 minutes, and add salt and pepper to taste.
5. Spoon onto dishes and serve.

Nutritional Value

- Calories: 187
- Fat: 2 grams
- Carbohydrates: 35 grams
- Fiber: 5 grams
- Protein: 8 grams

Delightful Veggie Pot Pie

(Preparation time: 3-4 hours/Serves: 6 servings)

Ingredients

- 6 -7 cups of chopped veggies of your choice
- ½ cup of diced onions
- 4 cloves of minced garlic
- Fresh thyme, finely chopped
- ½ cup of flour
- 2 cups of chicken broth
- ¼ cup of cornstarch
- ¼ cup of heavy cream
- Salt and pepper
- 1 thawed frozen puff pastry sheet
- 2 tablespoons of butter

Directions

1. Add the chopped veggies to the slow cooker as well as the garlic and onions.
2. Add the flour.
3. Add the broth and stir until everything is well blended.
4. Cover and cook for 3-4 hours on high.
5. In a small bowl, combine the cornstarch and ¼ cup of water and whisk together thoroughly. Add the cornstarch mix to the slow cooker.
6. Add the cream, cover and continue to cook until the mixture thickens, approximately 15 minutes.
7. Transfer the vegetable mixture into a baking dish.
8. Lay the puff pastry over the top.
9. Melt the butter and brush it over the top of the pastry.
10. Bake at 350 degrees for 10 minutes until the pastry turns fluffy and golden. Divide onto dishes and serve

Nutritional Value

- Calories: 325
- Fat: 0.8 grams
- Protein: 4.5 grams
- Carbohydrates: 6.7 grams

Graceful Dessert Recipes

Tasty Apple and Cranberry Dessert

(Preparation time: 3 hours/Serves: 4 servings)

Ingredients

- 4 medium sized sliced apples
- 1 cup of frozen or fresh cranberries
- 1 teaspoon of vanilla
- 8 tablespoons of light brown packed sugar
- 2 teaspoons of ground cinnamon, divided
- 1 packet of supermoist yellow cake mix, 15 ounces
- 8 tablespoons of melted butter
- Whipped cream

Directions

1. Grease the slow cooker.
2. Add 1 teaspoon of cinnamon, brown sugar, apples and cranberries to the slow cooker and combine them.
3. In a large bowl, combine the remaining 1 teaspoon of cinnamon with the dry cake mix.
4. Spread the mixture onto the fruits and drizzle the melted butter over the top. Cover and cook for 3 hours on high.
5. Spoon into bowls and serve with whipped cream.

Nutrition Values

- Calories: 230
- Fat: 12 grams
- Protein: 30 grams
- Carbohydrates: 4.5 grams

Caramel Pecan Pudding

(Preparation time: 3 hours: Serves: 4 servings)

Ingredients

- 1 ½ cups of Bisquick mix
- 16 tablespoons of sugar, divided
- 8 tablespoons of unsweetened baking cocoa
- 8 tablespoons of milk
- 12 tablespoons of caramel topping, divided
- 1 2/3 cups of hot water
- ½ cup of chopped pecans

Directions

1. In a large bowl, combine the Bisquick mix, 8 tablespoons of sugar, cocoa, milk and 6 tablespoons of caramel. Mix together thoroughly.
2. Pour the mixture into a slow cooker.
3. Add the hot water.
4. Top with the remaining sugar.
5. Cover and cook on low for 3 hours.
6. Divide into bowls, spread the remaining caramel over the top, sprinkle with pecans and serve.

Nutritional Value

- Carbohydrates: 19 grams
- Calories: 544
- Fat: 5.6 grams
- Protein: 3.4 grams

Mouth-Watering Chocolate Cake

(Preparation time:3.5 hours/Serves: 4 servings)

Ingredients

- 1 ½ cups of almond flour
- ¾ cup of granulated sugar or a sweetener of your preference
- 2/3 cup of cocoa powder
- ¼ cup of whey protein powder
- 2 teaspoons of baking powder
- ¼ teaspoons of salt
- ½ cup of melted butter
- 4 large eggs
- ¾ cup of unsweetened almond milk
- 1 teaspoon of vanilla extract
- Whipped cream

Directions

1. Combine the dry ingredients in a large bowl.
2. Add the wet ingredients to the dry ingredients one at a time, stirring as you go along. Whisk together thoroughly.
3. Grease the slow cooker and add the cake mixture.
4. Cover and cook for 3.5 hours on low.
5. Divide into bowls and serve with whipped cream.

Nutritional Values

- Calories: 260
- Fat: 14 grams
- Protein: 8 grams
- Carbohydrates: 15 grams

Fabulous Peanut Vanilla Chocolate Butter Cake

(Preparation time:4 hours/Serves: 4 servings)

Ingredients

- 3/4 cup of melted natural peanut butter
- 4 large eggs
- 2 cups of almond flour
- ½ a cup of water
- ¼ cup of unflavored whey protein powder
- ½ cup of melted butter
- 2 ounces of melted dark chocolate, sugar free
- ¾ cup of your preferred sweetener
- ¼ cup of coconut flour
- 1 teaspoon of vanilla extract
- 1 tablespoon of baking powder
- ¼ teaspoon of salt
- 1 teaspoon of vanilla extract

Directions

1. Grease the inside of the slow cooker with butter.
2. Combine all the ingredients in a large bowl and whisk together thoroughly.
3. Spoon 2/3 of the batter onto the base of the slow cooker.
4. Add half of the melted chocolate.
5. Add the remainder of the batter.
6. Add the remainder of the chocolate on top.
7. Cover and cook for 4 hours.
8. Divide onto plates and serve.

Nutritional Values

- Calories: 335
- Carbohydrates: 11.5 grams
- Fat: 27 grams
- Fiber: 5.2 grams
- Protein: 8 grams

Poppy Seed Butter Cake

(Preparation time: 3 hours/Serves: 4 servings)

Ingredients

- 4 large eggs
- The zest and juice of 4 lemons
- ½ cup of melted butter
- 2 cups of almond flour
- 3 tablespoons of poppy seeds
- 2 tablespoons of baking powder
- 1 tablespoon of vanilla extract
- 1 teaspoon of salt
- ½ cup of vanilla protein powder
- 3 tablespoons of vanilla protein powder
- ½ cup of xylitol

Directions

1. In a large bowl, combine all ingredients except the eggs and stir together thoroughly.
2. Add the eggs one by one and whisk together thoroughly.
3. Grease the slow cooker with butter.
4. Pour the batter into the slow cooker.
5. Cover and cook for 3 hours.
6. Divide onto plates and serve.

Nutritional Values

- Calories: 143
- Carbohydrates: 9 grams
- Fat: 10 grams
- Fiber: 1 gram
- Protein: 6 grams

Wonderful Raspberry Almond Cake

(Preparation time: 3 hours/Serves: 4 servings)

Ingredients

- 1 cup of fresh raspberries
- 1/3 cup of dark chocolate chips, sugar free
- 2 cups of almond flour
- 1 teaspoon of coconut extract
- ¾ cup of almond milk
- 4 large eggs
- 2 teaspoons of baking soda
- ¼ teaspoon of salt
- 1 cup of Swerve
- ½ cup of melted coconut oil
- 1 cup of shredded coconut unsweetened
- ¼ cup of powdered egg whites
- Butter for greasing

Directions

1. Grease the slow cooker with butter.
2. In a large bowl, combine all the ingredients and mix together thoroughly.
3. Pour the batter into the slow cooker.
4. Cover and cook for 3 hours on low.

Nutritional Values

- Calories: 362
- Carbohydrates: 12.8 grams
- Fat: 26 grams
- Protein: 8 grams

Scrumptious Chocolate Cocoa Cake

(Preparation time: 4 hours/Serves: 4 servings)

Ingredients

- 1 ½ cups of ground almonds
- ½ cup of coconut flakes
- 6 tablespoons of your preferred sweetener
- 2 teaspoons of baking powder
- A pinch of salt
- ½ cup of coconut oil
- ½ cup of cooking cream
- 2 tablespoons of lemon juice
- The zest from 2 lemons
- 2 large eggs
- Espresso and whipped cream for serving

Ingredients For The Topping

- 3 tablespoons of sweetener
- ½ a cup of boiling water
- 2 tablespoons of lemon juice
- 2 tablespoons of coconut oil

Directions

1. Combine the baking powder, sweetener, coconut and almonds in a large bowl. Whisk together thoroughly.
2. In another bowl, combine the eggs, juice, coconut oil and whisk together thoroughly.
3. Combine the wet and the dry ingredients and whisk together thoroughly.
4. Place aluminium foil on the bottom of the slow cooker.
5. Pour the batter into the slow cooker.
6. In a small bowl, combine the ingredients for the topping, combine together thoroughly and pour on top of the cake batter.
7. Cover the top of the slow cooker with paper towels to absorb condensation. Cover and cook for 3 hours on high.
8. Divide into bowls and serve with espresso and whipped cream.

Nutritional Values

Carbs: 5 grams, Protein: 7 grams, Fat: 24 grams, Calories: 310 grams

Conclusion

Thank you for purchasing my book! I hope you have found plenty of slow cooker recipes that you can incorporate into your daily diet. Remember, you don't have to stick to the exact recipes; you can mix the ingredients around and experiment until you find a dish that you prefer.

This is just the beginning of your slow cooker ketogenic diet journey. There are so many different recipes to make, but unfortunately there isn't enough space to put them all here. However, that shouldn't stop you from doing your own research, getting creative, and inventing your own recipes.

I wish you all the best in your life of healthy eating!

Free Bonus: 7 Days Ketogenic Diet Meal Plan

Shopping List

Ground sausage	Whipping cream	Chicken breast
Onion	Butter or lard	Minced lean ground pork
Dried Parsley	Cheddar cheese	2 cans Italian diced tomatoes
Garlic powder	Green bell peppers	Dry basil
Thyme	Ham	Lemons
Bacon	Fresh spinach	Whole chicken
Chicken broth	Eggplants	Pork ribs
Red bell peppers	Olive oil	Vinegar
Parmesan cheese	Spicy pork sausage	Worcestershire sauce
Heavy white cream	Italian diced tomatoes	Dry mustard
Mushrooms	Tomato paste	Chili powder
Salt	Mozzarella cheese	Ground cumin
Black pepper	Unsweetened almond milk	Boneless, skinless chicken
Zucchini	Spinach	2 cans of diced tomatoes
Ground walnuts	Artichoke hearts	Balsamic vinegar
Ground almonds	Garlic	Dried oregano
Coconut flakes	Coconut flour	Dried rosemary
Cinnamon	Cooked boneless ham	Whole pork tenderloin
Baking soda	Maple syrup	Sweet onions
Baking powder	Honey Dijon mustard	Bay leaf
Eggs	Packed brown sugar	Ground cloves
Coconut oil	Sour cream	Roasted red peppers
Sweetener	Chicken stock	Black olives
Vanilla	Can of diced green chilis and tomatoes	Reduced-fat feta cheese

Cauliflower	Homemade taco seasoning	Dried oregano
Cream cheese	Low sodium chicken broth	Pork shoulder
Tomato paste	1 can of light beer	Broccoli
Coconut milk	Red pepper flakes	Frozen cauliflower
White wine	Pork shoulder	Grated cheddar cheese
Turmeric	Yellow onion	Onion powder
Ginger powder	Italian seasoning	Apples
Curry powder	Turkey pepperoni	Fresh or frozen cranberries
Paprika	Crushed fennel seeds	Supermoist yellow cake mix
Pork sirloin chops on the bone	Cod	Whipped cream
Limes	Shrimp	Bisquick mix
Ground cumin	Oxtail	Sugar
Frozen turkey meatballs	Red onion	Unsweetened baking cocoa
Bottled yellow and red sweet peppers	Ground cardamom	Caramel topping
Crushed red peppers	Ground coriander seeds	Chopped pecans
Reduced sodium pasta sauce	Beef broth	Almond flour
Fresh basil	Small turnips	Unsweetened almond milk
Vanilla extract	Xylitol	Shredded unsweetened coconut
Natural peanut butter	Fresh raspberries	Powdered egg whites
Sugar free dark chocolate	Dark chocolate chips	Ground almonds
Poppy seeds	Coconut extract	Cooking cream
Vanilla protein powder	Swerve	Espresso

Meal Plan

Day 1	**Total Count:** • Calories: 726 • Fat: 44.5 grams • Carbohydrates: 65.2 grams • Protein: 74.7 grams
Breakfast	**Beautiful Mushroom Bacon Breakfast** • Calories: 166 • Fat: 15.5 grams • Carbohydrates: 2.1 grams • Protein: 6.7 grams
Lunch	**Amazing Sour Cream Chicken** • Calories: 262 • Fat: 13 grams • Carbohydrates: 23 grams • Protein: 32 grams
Dinner	**Delightful Turkey Basil Meatballs** • Calories: 68 • Fat: 4 grams • Carbohydrates: 3 grams • Protein: 6 grams
Dessert	**Tasty Apple and Cranberry Dessert** • Calories: 230 • Fat: 12 grams • Carbohydrates: 4.5 grams • Protein: 30 grams
Day 2	**Total Count:** • Calories: 1291 • Fat: 56.6 grams • Carbohydrates: 33 grams • Protein: 59.4 grams
Breakfast	**Delicious Zucchini Cinnamon Nut Bread** • Calories: 210 • Fat: 18 grams • Carbohydrates: 4 grams • Protein: 5 grams

Lunch	**Mouth Watering Minced Pork Zucchini Lasagne** • Calories: 398 • Fat: 30 grams • Carbohydrates: 10 grams • Protein: 23 grams
Dinner	**Wonderful Weekend Chicken Cooked with Beer** • Calories: 139 • Fat: 3 grams • Carbohydrates: 0 grams • Protein: 28 grams
Dessert	**Caramel Pecan Pudding** • Calories: 544 • Fat: 5.6 grams • Carbohydrates: 19 grams • Protein: 3.4 grams
Day 3	**Total Count:** • Calories: 1063 • Fat: 66 grams • Carbohydrates: 26 grams • Protein: 61 grams
Breakfast	**Mouth-Watering Cauliflower & Cheese Bake** • Calories: 232 • Fat: 20 grams • Carbohydrates: 3 grams • Protein: 11 grams
Lunch	**Fantastic Lemon Thyme Chicken** • Calories: 120 • Fat: 8 grams • Carbohydrates: 1 gram • Protein: 12 grams
Dinner	**Delightful Coconut, Turmeric Pork Curry** • Calories: 451 • Fat: 24 grams • Carbohydrates: 7 grams • Protein: 30 grams

Dessert	**Mouth-Watering Chocolate Cake** • Calories: 260 • Fat: 14 grams • Carbohydrates: 15 grams • Protein: 8 grams
Day 4	**Total Count:** • Calories: 1161 • Fat: 71.9 grams • Carbohydrates: 31.3 grams • Protein: 103.6 grams
Breakfast	**Spectacular Ham and Spinach Frittata** • Calories: 109 • Fat: 6.9 grams • Carbohydrates: 1.8 grams • Protein: 5.6 grams
Lunch	**Beautiful BBQ Ribs** • Calories: 410 • Fat: 28 grams • Carbohydrates: 14 grams • Protein: 38 grams
Dinner	**Beautiful Italian Black Olive Chicken** • Calories: 307 • Fat: 10 grams • Carbohydrates: 4 grams • Protein: 52 grams
Dessert	**Fabulous Peanut Vanilla Chocolate Butter Cake** • Calories: 335 • Fat: 27 grams • Carbohydrates: 11.5 grams • Protein: 8 grams
Day 5	**Total Count:** • Calories: 979 • Fat: 53 grams • Carbohydrates: 29 grams • Protein: 83 grams

Breakfast	**Tasty Sausage & Eggplant Bake** • Calories: 210 • Fat: 12 grams • Carbohydrates: 6 grams • Protein: 15 grams
Lunch	**Delightful Balsamic Oregano Chicken** • Calories: 190 • Fat: 6 grams • Carbohydrates: 5 grams • Protein: 26 grams
Dinner	**Spectacular One Pot Special Meal** • Calories: 436 • Fat: 25 grams • Carbohydrates: 9 grams • Protein: 36 grams
Dessert	**Poppy Seed Butter Cake** • Calories: 143 • Fat: 10 grams • Carbohydrates: 9 grams • Protein: 6 grams
Day 6	**Total Count:** • Calories: 1434 • Fat: 94.1 grams • Carbohydrates: grams • Protein: 81.2 grams
Breakfast	**Artichoke Hearts Bake** • Calories: 141 • Fat: 7.1 grams • Carbohydrates: 3.8 grams • Protein: 10 grams
Lunch	**Scrumptious Bay Leaf Pork Roast Shoulder** • Calories: 421 • Fat: 30 grams • Carbohydrates: 10 grams • Protein: 33 grams

Dinner	**Cinnamon, Coriander, Broccoli Oxtail Pot** • Calories: 510 • Fat: 31 grams • Carbohydrates: 14 grams • Protein: 68 grams
Dessert	**Wonderful Raspberry Almond Cake** • Calories: 362 • Fat: 26 grams • Carbohydrates: 12.8 grams • Protein: 8 grams
Day 7	**Total Count:** • Calories: 1282 • Fat: 75.6 grams • Carbohydrates: grams • Protein: 39.5 grams
Breakfast	**Sweet Ham Maple Breakfast** • Calories: 430 • Fat: 24 grams • Carbohydrates: 23 grams • Protein: 32 grams
Lunch	**Tantalizing Chicken Breast with Artichoke Stuffing** • Calories: 222 • Fat: 7 grams • Carbohydrates: 4 grams • Protein: 52 grams
Dinner	**Tasty Ham and Cauliflower Stew** • Calories: 320 • Fat: 20.6 grams • Carbohydrates: 7.5 grams • Protein: 23.3 grams
Dessert	**Scrumptious Chocolate Cocoa Cake** • Calories: 310 • Fat: 24 grams • Carbohydrates: 5 grams • Protein: 7 grams